The Poems Of Eileen Powell:
(A Lifetime of Poetry)
by
Eileen Powell

136 PAGES

A *Lost & Found* Book
Published by
Newfoundland Press

ISBN: 978-1-927046-27-2

Newfoundland Press Edition - Eileen Powell ©2013

New
Found
Land
Press

This Book is dedicated to my Parents:

Newman Gough
(June 10, 1896 - Feb. 16, 1986)

&
Alice (Stead) Gough
(Aug. 31, 1898 - March 15, 1976)

The Poems Of Eileen Powell:
(A Lifetime of Poetry)

by

Eileen Powell

New
Found
Land
Press

Prologue

M Y Aunt Eileen...

...I know her from Laite's Lane, where I ran to play with my
cousins in Corner Brook. And I noticed that she had a certain
look. What that look was, I didn't totally recognize myself, until
years spun me far away from my childhood and into poetry. I
walked into the dark shadows of San Fernando Valley to find
my natural home as a Newfoundland poet of my own variety.

In her look, even as I remember it from childhood, I had a
sense that Aunt Eileen was always in two worlds at once. What
she saw, heard and felt, was recorded to emerge as a poem, in
the web of observation & connection of her perception. That
combined with the necessary other part of this strange dual-
vision - the *everyday* world in all its wonder-filled reality, and
yet as ephemeral as all our lives. Caught like leaves upon the
stream – we trade stories until we are dragged along spinning
and supported by our yarns ...

... I could see that the mother of Diane, of Marilyn, of Linda,
of Jim and of David was a Poet. She saw her children in the
context of an Epic Poem that allows all directions. She is, like
most writers, a Jill-of-all-trades in her thinking life. A wonder-

fueled mother, a Nurse who saw death and destruction play across the wards in the way that it moves, giving wisdom as we learn how much may be lost, and yet how much may be endured.

Writers' words help us heal, become our Nurses. They give us a place to speak the truth; to listen to one's heart as closely as one listens to a small child.

She has the ear of a Burke, can sing her own tunes, will sit at a Hammond Chord organ and play what she's thinking. She takes on inept politicians and slams whole Political Parties with a song. This edition now includes some samples of her other work. And humour.

In her work I also see her Mother, my grandmother Alice, who also had the main trait of a poet – the ability to allow *all* into the circle. There were, and are, for Eileen Powell no 'them'; her faith is the faith of a poet: that, having heard the necessary story, we will be moved to action. Like me, she knows the way of the tea-leaves, and how she and her mother could envision in the swirl-and-blur a reflection of life projected upon a cloud.

And she learned from Newman, her father – a natural-born, and war-warped writer himself. His letters home, the diaries he kept, the love he had for books, and the ways he could take them apart and repair & rebuild them – allowed me to run a press, take a book apart and look at the glorious text and space, nesting all our thoughts.

The true lineage of a poet is not what we studied in Literature, but what happened at home, in the small Infinite world of childhood, with neighbors, friends, simple trips to the store, a letter from a distant friend. It's what we learn in life – for there were poets long, long before there were schools.

No wonder she became a poet. She apprenticed to the trade of writing through *writing* itself. She wrote poems for others who helped the ill and dying; she loved buckling her verse for Political satires; making quick observations & long-lived observations showing how the years change us, how shadow advances while eating light; how sparks emerge from shadows. Eileen Powell became a working poet. Could easily have moved into the exalted category of *Anon*. However, because the Guttenberg Press is now back, churning & grinding & sparking & running out of fuel & being re-fueled by imagination & wit & fun & compassion & anger, and a central stillness, writers have to hear all of a story. All of it. Not leaving anything out...

...So in 1947 she sang of being a Nurse, of hearing the call of Florence Nightingale. She went to work – amongst the first of modern women in those far-off times to go back to work, to do whatever a man could do – she walked into that and it sits well on her.

She has the open eye and ear of the Poet. She was trained by her Mother to ignore the superficial costumes; to see the truth – that we all are equal. Nan Gough's view was also clear - if you have something & someone needs it – why not give it at once? Poets have been known to give away our poems, to donate our lives: trading years for something as simple as a lucid observation. Who wouldn't?

My Partner in this press & all life, Caren Moon, knew that Aunt Eileen was a poet. Caren loved her poems, and we talked about it, and then the magical arrival of a packet in the mail – Sent to us by Eileen's daughter, Marilyn. It was magical as poem after poem after poem emerged. We read them, passed them back and forth, told each other what our favorites were, and then discovered weeks later that they were *all* our favorites.

This book reveals only some of Eileen Powell's writing. She has penned letters to the editor, and never had a hesitation to call it as she sees it; to be relentless with the truth. She scribbled on note paper, envelopes, shopping lists, journals, paper napkins. And the poems included work from her youth in 1943, so I've now met Aunt Eileen before my own birth. I was sung to by this poet when she baby-sat me, and had poems recited to me by my mother & father at home, and the word-swirl surrounded me, like the ribbons on the Scepter in Cape St. George when they dance '*Septs & Huits.*'

You're in for a treat; here you may read her love poems, her poems at home, her early loves, her writing now & her writing in the eternal '*then.*' This Poet is a fierce & wonderful knitter as well. In knitting, she flings together a freeform loop and draws the yarn towards her; she always works with her own pattern. Whatever yarn is furnished, why, she can knit it into mitts. When trouble & sadness drop the very gut to the floor she can knit it all into a yarn; a poem.

Caren & I have followed a simple progression in this book, suggested by the poems themselves, where Eileen Powell takes us through the Dawn, into all seasons right to the close of Winter, and then, as if an imprint on the snow, her voice hooks echoes & holds them till they melt. With everyday voices; with what she sees in daily life, how she lives it, and where she now stands with her poetic powers in hand, she holds the pages towards us and they drift like snow across the rooms we all remember. A dusting of the future.

The approach in our press is to let writers write as they know how to do...with minimum interference from Publisher. Same this time. Now's the time for us to stand aside and introduce to you a Poet...

                    ... *The Poems of Eileen Powell.*

Dawn

Dawn

What Joy ... What happiness
To wake and see the sun
Shooting little rays of light
Across my room, and on my face
Oh Glorious Dawn!

Spider

Do you see the spider on the wall
    In the hall?
He's lying very still
    But I know he will move to and fro
    All night long
As soon as Mom and Dad go.

They leave the light on
    In the hall
Just for me, so I can see
When I get up at night
So I won't get a fright.

So I just watch my spider
Going to and fro, side to side,
Spinning a web, that's made of silk
    Shining in the sun.
But when it's dark, I want to hide
Being in the dark alone
Just isn't fun.

For The Children

Just simple poems for everyone to understand,

No dictionary words, that sometimes make you wonder

What it's all about . . . . . .

Written and thought of in so many places,

In so many moods, maybe looking at the Autumn woods

And skies, and all your happy faces,

Or thinking of the past. And long ago memories

Of maybe happier times that flew so fast.

But all these rhymes are coming from the heart

In which each one of you has played some little part.

Spring:

Spring

At last it feels like Spring
The robins on the dried out grass
Raising their heads to sing
Now that April days are past.

The sounds of little Children
Happy to be outside again.
Playing games and having fun
Coats and hats, tossed happily aside
Enjoying every moment in the sun
Flowers peeping through the ground
Purple, white, of different hue.
Leaves spreading wide, and sounds
Of buzzing all around
And shining sun in a sky of Azure Blue.

The Infirmary Walls

(1947)

The Infirmary walls will always hold
Voices of Nurses, brave not bold
Who struggle on for greater things
Becoming angels without wings.
Each cap, a halo round her head
Shines upon some sufferer's bed,
Who reaches out a hand to find
Being held by another, oh, so kind.

Their weary hearts they try to hide
While, they themselves, begin to guide
Some patient back to health again
And help ease someone else's pain.
They smile, and talk and then smooth out
A trouble that made someone pout.
There's healing in their very touch
They think that no great task is much.

We throw our torch, to you behind
And pray that you will never find
It hard to hold – and keep it high;
Don't say "I can't" but "do or die."
The goal is near and can be won,
By you, whose work is just begun.
Be patient, kind and you won't fail
To be a Florence Nightingale.

They Walked The Paths...

They walked the paths where lovers trod
To watch the stars above
He put his arms around her then
A boy and girl in love.

The flowers nodded as they passed
As if to say, "we know."
The tears fell swiftly down her cheeks
She could not stop the flow

For she was just a country girl
And he a city boy
His parents never liked her
And he, their pride and joy.

The night he told her they must part
She thought her heart would break
He told her that his love for her
Was really a mistake.

Many years have passed – she sits alone
Watching the stars above
But the memory never leaves her
Of the boy and girl in love.

Baby Girl

When you were just a baby girl
I held you to my breast.
How could anything so small
Make me feel so blest?
Tiny little hands and feet
Eyes so shiny blue,
Not much hair; but oh so sweet,
And, Oh, how I loved you.

Our Little Boy

Dear little boy so small and sweet
You captured all our love
Such tiny little hands and feet
God sent you from above.
One day you're just a baby boy
Reaching tiny hands, to touch
My cheeks or nose, oh what joy
To have someone to love so much.

Then, you're only one year old
And taking tiny steps to me
Trying to be oh so bold
Not old enough for me to free.

Then two, a little braver now
Running in the summer sun
Laughing at new things you see
Having so much fun.

You're long past three, and then you're four
I'm sure I run a mile
Each day, making sure you're safe
And see that winning smile.

Then you're five and off to school
Just look, how you have grown.
With unshed tears , I watch you go
Leaving me alone.

Lost Love

You came so like a breath of spring
　　into my life,
Asking me to share your dreams
　　And be your wife

I had so much love to give
And felt so happy,
　　Just to live
For you, and make you happy
　　every day.
But you, not knowing,
　　Threw it all away.

Just little things at first;
Not being there
when needed ,
　　Was the worst.

The times you just left,
And went your way
The children needed me
What could I say?

I couldn't always walk
    Out through the door
        When things got rough
            I couldn't love you more

Than I did, and though we had
    Disagreements many
I never said
        I didn't love you, or showed regret,
        Because we hadn't any

Money, for the outside life and Pleasure
    You should have known
        I didn't measure
Love by material things and so

I only want to let you know
Love is shown by little things you do.
A stolen glance,
        A touch of hands, when you
        Think no one else can see
Just being kind and thoughtful,
            Making me
Feel loved and wanted,
            nothing more.

You wouldn't take the time to see

The wealth we had in store

You never knew the hours

       You made me grieve

So, now, with Love behind me

It's my turn to leave.

Only Five

Such a tiny life
    Our first little girl
        To love and cherish, and to show
            How much we love her
                And try to give the World.

Then a little boy
    So soon after
        A Father's Joy
            To have a son
                To follow in his steps and do
                    All the things he should have done.

Another girl
    To bring more joy,
        And then, another baby boy
            The house seems overflowing
                With so much chatter
                    And tiny feet, that pitter patter.

Another baby girl
        To keep me on my toes
                The days just fly,
                        I wonder where time goes?

And then the years fly, and
        One by one they leave
                And I am left alone and wondering
                        When did the years go by?

I haven't had the time to see
        The grey streaks in my hair,
                Or see Old Father Time
                        Put wrinkles here and there.

The Happy times and early years
        Went by so fast,
                With hardly time to breathe
                        And now at last

I've time to read a book and do
        The things I never had the time before
                But Oh!
                        What loneliness at times

No one needs me now

To kiss the tears away or

Wipe a runny nose,

No one to run in after school

And say "Where's Mom?"

No one to tuck in bed

Or hug me tight

And after prayers are said

No one to say "I love you, Mommy"

With a kiss Goodnight.

If I could Only Tell The World

If I could only tell the world how much I love you.

If I could only tell the world how much I care,

But you belong to someone new, and I'm here all alone

With only broken dreams and memories to share.

I was the first love in your life, you always told me

I had the world and all your love, to see me through,

Now you're someone else's love, your arms won't hold me

I should have realized my life was there with you.

I left you all alone, so many lonely nights
My heart began to roam, when you turned out the lights
I know I was untrue, but you put up with me
And then one day you said, "I'm setting your heart free."

Now I have lonely days and nights without your love dear,
I'm paying for the hours I left you all alone,
And I can never tell the world how much I miss you
Or tell you, how I love you darling. Please come home.

Scent Of Lilacs

When I forget the scent of lilacs in the Spring
Or new mown hay that permeates the air
The day I do not hear the Robins' sing
Or choral voices sending words of prayer
When I don't recall my children's happy smiles
That light their faces, showing all their love;
I'm not aware of summer sun, and azure skies;
Of walking barefoot in the grass below
And myriads of color that possess the Fall and you.
When I can only feel the Winter and its cold
Then you will know
That I am old.

Spring

Oh wondrous Spring
    At last birds sing
And flowers bloom
    Little birds are singing everywhere
So much to share
    A world so beautiful ... All Nature free
Because God shared his gifts
    With you and me.

The Night We Met

I can't forget the night we met
The first time I saw you,
I looked into your eyes and then
I fell in love with you.

I wonder if you felt the way
I did ... You held my hand
And then, my dear, I knew my heart
Was then in your command.

We went together for six months
Then you left without a word,
I often wondered why, my love,
And then I found you'd heard,

And listened to a lot of things
You should have known were lies,
I felt so blue, Oh surely you
Could not mean those Goodbyes.

We're back together once again
I hope you'll never leave,
But if you do, I'll always wear
My heart upon my sleeve.

Daydreaming

(A poem without rhyme)

Bees buzzing by the classroom window,
    Sun shining in our faces. Oh so warm and bright,
Lessons forgotten for the moment,
    And dreams take over, while we are lost
        In Adventure.

Tom Sawyer ... barefoot and paddling up the River
    On his makeshift raft, and sounds of children's laughter
Shouting in the distance,
    On Robinson Crusoe on his lonely Island,
No one to bother, just to roam across the forest green.

Birds singing, and the smell of blooming flowers,
    Lost in dreams and reveries, when suddenly
We're coming back,
    Back to reality and the voice of teacher
Asking "Will you please explain what I've been saying, John?"

Memories

Childhood memories are so sweet
    Like honeysuckle to the bee,
Remembering days that were so summer long,
    And winter nights that were so endless,
It's so sweet remembering days that used to be.

All summer long just having fun
    No lessons to be learned,
Swimming in the old town pool
    Happy just walking barefoot in the sand,

Or lying in the grass and
    Starting at the passing clouds,
Those chariots and horses racing
    Across the sky,
            What pleasant Reveries for me.

Summer

To Marilyn

Dear little girl with
Those beautiful eyes
Twinkling with laughter
And blue as the skies
You bring so much Happiness
Into our lives
Just watching you play
Is another Sunrise!

Waiting

She sits and waits beside the gate
Of memories fond and true,
She's waiting all alone tonight
Thinking only of you.

For 'twas not very long ago
When you were by her side,
You whispered love songs in her ear
For soon she'd be your bride.

And when you left her, all her vows
And dreams of love were shattered,
Her wedding veil was put away
For those things did not matter.

Each night she sits and waits for you
Altho' your paths did sever,
And even though you were untrue
She'll wait for you forever.

Bark Of Destiny

Sail on ... Oh Bark of Destiny,
Your topsails shot with fire.
Sail on into the land of Dreams
The dreams we all desire.

And as you travel on the foam
Of waters calm and bright,
You take with you our message
To lead you safe aright.

You've sailed the Seven Seas of Life
And shared with us our grief,
You've helped us in our time of strife
And to us brought relief.

You bring glad tidings to each Port
And soothe each restless wave,
These treasures found in every land
Are Treasures we all crave.

Dear Mom

Dear Mom:
   You will never know
   The way I miss you
   The way that I long, and yearn to kiss you
   Last night in my sleep, I saw an image of you standing by me.

Dear Mom:
   The way that you smile
   The brown of your hair,
   The silver therein caused by worry and care
   I see you sitting in your old rocking chair
   Like an Angel.

Dear Mom:

   I long to see you more

   Than ever before,

   Only now I know I used to grieve you so

   When I thought you were sleeping

   You were quietly weeping.

Dear Mom:

   I just can't forget

   That day I went

   Away from your love

   I know what it meant

   To leave you alone Darling Mother of mine,

   Don't ever leave me;

         Dear Mom.

Love Gone

The days seem long
    The hours drag past,
The love I thought would always last
    Is Gone.

I loved you so
    I thought you knew,
I guess I should have known that you
    Would Go.

The way I feel
    About your kiss,
I can't believe, my darling, this
    Is Real.

The love we knew
    The kiss we tried,
I never felt that someday I'd
    Feel Blue.

A Hymn

I'd like to be a friend of Jesus
I'd like to follow in the paths his feet have trod.
If I could hold his hand in mind and follow
I know I'll see the wondrous works of GOD.

I know that he will understand me
And be forgiving for the sins that I have done,
And where the verdant pastures grow, I know He'll lead me
And find the Promised Land, Our rising sun.

Into the Garden of Gethsemane, he'll lead me,
And there together we will humbly kneel in prayer.
He'll hold my hand and to the Promised Land we'll wander
And all our loved ones will be waiting there.

Gethsemane will be the answer
To all the prayers that I have never said before,
And if he hears me I'll be happy
I couldn't ask for any more.

My cares will fade away, my burdens will be lifted
And I'll be happier than I have been before,
My cup will overflow, and I will be so gifted
To live within his house for evermore.

Is This You?

The little things you do and say
   Reflect your inner self and in a way
      Tell so many things about the way
         You feel inside.

Trying so hard to please your "stranger" friends
   And, by doing so, hide
      The love you could be sharing
         With the ones who really love you
            And are *Always* caring.

Bless Me Lord

Out of bed the same old time
Every morning rain or shine
Breakfast, then the same routine
Just another damn machine

Cleaning floors, dusting chairs

Running up and down the stairs

Clothes to wash, beds to make

Then it's time to start to bake

Getting dinner on the table

Washing dishes when I'm able.

.

Afternoon, that much is done

Is there any time for fun?

Time to do a little knitting,

But that damn phone knows I'M sitting,

"Up and at 'em" time for tea,

There's more dishes, "poor old me."

Then I'm getting supper ready

Housework keeps you working steady.

Have to keep things all in place,

Hardly time to wash my face.

Then at night, when work's all done???

T.V. shows are sometimes fun.

Midnight, and it's time for bed

Then my nightly prayer is said

"It's only me, Lord. Please don't panic,

Just Bless this old KITCHEN MECHANIC".

Invisible Me

Everything I do or say
        You magnify
Or turn around in such a way
To mean something
        I never had in mind to say

I try to say what's on my mind
    But you don't say a word
        Sometimes I'm neither here nor there
          Just speaking, never heard.

No matter what I do or say
    I just can't make you see
        That I'm still here beside you
        Poor Invisible me.

Nestled In The Valley

Nestled in the Valley
Surrounded by trees
A garden filled with flowers
And happy memories.

Summer sunshine falling on the ground
Making the grass and garden grow
Fresh flowers blooming all around
And listening to the summer sound
Bees humming, mixed with children's' laughs
No where, such beauty to be seen
Now or hereafter.

A tidy little house
A place I called home,
No happier place to me
Wherever I roamed.

All the happy years
Are past and long gone
But all the memories I love
Still linger on.

Invisibility

It doesn't mean that I'm not here
Or can't be touched
Although I feel, I can't be seen
By you at times -- it's so much
more than that.

It's just that left out feeling
Although we're here
The same four walls around us
But we 're not together - miles apart

Separated by some unknown barrier
That comes between us, more often now
'Why can't you see,
This feeling of being dead
while still alive
That's real INVISIBILITY.

We Live For Love Tonight

We live for love tonight
While you are here beside me.
    In the pale moonlight
The sudden summer breeze,
    That whispers through the trees
Tells me you're mine, and only mine tonight.

You're here within my arms,
And suddenly I'm overpowered
    By your charms
The touch of your soft hand
    Makes me feel twice the woman
And darling, I am yours, at your command.

We'll love beneath the stars
And if in ecstasy, we fly away to Mars.
    We'll leave the world behind
And stay where we can find
    True love forever, while we love tonight.

On Seeing You Again

I caught a glimpse of you today
And after all those years
I still felt the same old way
And had to stop the tears

I said I'd never shed for you
But, oh, how my heart lied
I knew I wouldn't speak to you
I couldn't if I tried.

And so I let you go your way
I kept out of your life.
You never knew that I was there
As you walked to meet your wife.

Because Of You

Because of you, my days
        Are filled with happiness
        The darkest night is bright
        The sky is filled with stars
        You fill my heart with song

Our love just can't go wrong

Just take my hand we'll fly

'To Jupiter or Mars.'

Grandmother's Visit

(Steven)

Happiness is looking up to see

A little face pressed against the window.

Eyes full of excitement

Looking straight at me.

And tiny feet running across the floor

Waiting breathlessly

Until I'm at the door.

Searching in my purse for some tiny treasure

And when it's found, smiling happily;

Then looking all around,

To see if he's been caught.

Nothing that I give, can measure,

To the love he's brought to me.

Everyday, he's finding something new
And, in his special way keeps occupied
So many things to do,
Always on the run,
Making laughter everywhere and having
So much fun.

I wouldn't miss my special visits,
Or change places with millionaires.
When the day of fun is over
And I'm in the rocking chair
With this tiny little boy, so full of love
So warm, nestled in my arms asleep
You can have everything else; but I'll keep this moment
As a memory that will live
Forever in this heart of mine, and I can say
Thank you God for giving
This little boy
Who has blessed and made my day.

To Madge

(Friendship)

1:

Friendship is like a garden,
>   Filled with flowers.
We must spend hours
>   Making them grow
Giving tender loving care
And then, when we are through
>   Maybe one will be
A friend like you.

2:
"Friendship is a plant that we must water often"
Friendship is like a garden
>   Filled with flowers
To make them grow
>   We must spend hours.

3:
And then, when we are through
Maybe there will be
A friend like you.

To Ashley

Your presence is just like a flower
Ready to unfold its leaves for me
And shed the cover, that surrounds
A Bloom, so beautiful to see.

Big blue eyes that look so deep
Into my own
The little wisps of hair around your face

And curls that spring and fly
Each time you run

When you smile
Your face lights up
And twinkling stars shine in your eyes.
Your laughter radiates a mile,
You're pretty as a buttercup.

Your heart is full of love you say
And every time I look at you
There is no doubt within my mind,
That what you say is true.

To Nanny Case

An angel smiled today
As she walked to you and took your hand
Leading you along the path
Where flowers bloomed so beautiful
Into your Promised Land.

I wasn't at your side
To hold your hand & help to ease your path.
You left before I had a chance
To see you once again.

I'll keep my memories of you so very dear
And hope you know how much
I'll miss you
Goodbye dear Friend.

To Wanda

(May 21/'92)

I met her just a year ago
Only a whisper of the girl she used to be
A young mother holding on to life
And things she held so dear.
One little boy, who hardly knew his mom
When she was well and full of life
And free from pain, that every day
She tried so hard to bear.

No one will ever know what she went through
Those lonely nights; so all alone
Wondering, when will all this end;
The pain, the suffering, the agony
Of knowing she may not see the dawn again.
She always talked about the future.
Even the long winter days, she spoke of Spring
And summer yet to come
When she would just lie in the Sun
And talk with friends. And laugh
And just have fun.

"Don't worry about me,
I'm going to be alright," she said,
"I'll best them yet, you'll see."
And we thought, "How brave she is, and strong
Was all that faith she had,
A front for all her friends?
When in her heart she knew
That she would soon be gone.

Behind Closed Doors

Behind closed doors, the shadows creep
And monsters hide
From all the world outside, but in this confine
They stand and keep their vigil
And control the mind.

Outside these walls, the monsters disappear
And all the Valiants that ever lived
Will suddenly take over
And other personalities surface and we hear
Compliments, sweet talk; no one ever knew we're there.

This other side is meant for Strangers

And they think, "this is perfection like a Story Book."

If they only had a chance to take another look

Inside the walls where suddenly Prince Valiant disappears

And the monster once again takes over

And begins his own demonical dance.

Dreams

Dreams are meant to be shared

By someone you love, who loves you

And cares about you.

Someone who wants to spend each day

Just making life worth living

Helping you to be yourself

Accepting you for what you are

Not as you would be.

Giving you room to breathe

    The air around you

Making you feel free, even when

    His arms surround you

Making you feel free.

Then all the dreams
You've ever had
Won't matter if they don't come true.
When someone cares, for you alone
    That someone shares
        Your biggest dreams with you.

Steven's Birthday

Happy Birthday, little one,
This is your special day.
Laugh and run, have lots of fun
On this your first birthday.

A little boy, brought so much joy
To every Mom and Dad
And, as you play, all through the day
You make their hearts so glad.

You have someone to hold you tight
And wipe away the tears
And tuck you in your bed at night
Banishing your tears.

Fall

Autumn

I think of Autumn and I see
    The leaves come tumbling down,
I see the summer lose its robe
    And wear a golden crown.

The leaves go gliding all around
    Of every different hue,
The trees stand, silhouetted bare
    Beside a sky so blue.

The golden maple always holds
    A thrill for every heart,
Everything at Autumn seems
    To play a Magic part.

The little streamlet flows along
    Beside the grassy mound,
The trees cast shadows everywhere
    There's so much beauty found.

In every lake, in every tree
    Oh wondrous Gifts of Nature,
Spread all around for you and me,
    The work of our Creator.

My Kitchen

My kitchen is my very own
A place to spend my time alone
Preparing meals, and God knows what.
I know each corner – every pot,
My recipes from way back when
I was a young bride, learning then,
To cook like Mom, and wished I could
Make bread like hers – then – we used wood
To keep a steady hand, to bake
These recipes I loved to make.

To Betty - Sept 6th /82

You've lost someone who was so very dear
    And at this moment life is empty and forlorn,
You just can't seem to bear
    The heavy burden life has thrown
Upon you, leaving you so all alone.

But life goes on, and you must learn
    To face each new tomorrow with a smile,
No need to sit and yearn about the past,
    But all the while
Remembering all the happy hours
    You spent together,
These memories will always last.

I Remember

(1943)

We met in crisp September
When the leaves began to fall,
We made a pledge together
When we heard the canyon call.

A week was spent in gaiety
And then, that Autumn day,
We said "Good-Bye" amid my tears
You wanted it that way.

But I will still remember
Your lips, your dark brown hair,
That night beneath the starry sky
When we first learned to care.

No one can ever ease the pain
That comes, because we had to part,
No changes, no mountain full of years
Can take your image
From my Heart.

Bittersweet

A Victory won, or so I thought
At last I've given him, the same as he gives me,
All the years of never being brought
    A tiny gift, a card,
Or just a Happy Birthday, an Anniversary.

Today I didn't say "Happy Birthday"
As I did so many other years,
Why is it I feel just as sad
    As when I've been forgotten?
Through unshed tears I see
    That being silent was no Victory.

A Friend

I met a friend today.

Someone who had the time to pause

And smile, and pass the time of day,

To clasp my hand and say

"So nice to see you, Dear, again."

Making the world seem brighter, then

We waved and went each separate way.

Wandering Lonely

I too have wandered lonely

But only in dreams, not as the cloud

That travels hither and yon,

Seeing so many scenes and faces

And such wonderful places.

I've stayed, always by your side

Trying to make you understand

That my world means as much to me

As yours to you, and

Maybe even more, because I have

The memories of Happy times.

With babies learning how to walk and talk
And growing up and teaching them
The way to live,
But most of all to give
Happiness to those they love.

The days we have before us
Now are numbered
And we have so very few Happy moments
That we share,
Too many unimportant things
Make up our days, and there
Are so many hours of uninterrupted silence
Mingling between us.

The children have grown
And found their way of life
So we are left alone
To find ourselves again,
To share our memories together
In our "twilight years" or keeping silent
Never speaking from the heart
Keeping so much unsaid, watching
The love that once we knew
Destroyed, before we part.

To Mom

If only I could see you one more time
  To hold your hand ... to touch your face
    To feel your presence, see your sweet smile
    To know you Love again, a little while.

You always gave so much
  Your love, your time
    Never ending ... always helping
    Others bear the burdens of each day
      Ever cheerful, always happy
        As you traveled Life's Highway.

We took so much for granted
  Sometimes all too busy with each daily task
    Of raising families, trying to make a home,
      Never taking time to ask
        If you were feeling lonely and alone.

And now you're gone, there's no one
  To share the little joys
    Of grandchildren growing up
      And happy times
        Leaving us to wonder if you knew
          Our hidden feelings
          And how much we always loved you.

Time To Spare

Those many times
    I dreamed of hours
      To read so many books
        And then today
          With just one look
            Into the Mirror of my life, I saw
            The wrinkles I had never
          Had the time to see.
           The graying hair
            And then I knew
              There's no such thing
               As "Time To Spare."

Where Did We Go Wrong?
(Music 'Romeo & Juliet')

Where did we go wrong
  What happened to the love we shared
    When we were young?
      Those happy days when we walked
        Smiling in the sun
          Or just held hands and watched
            The rising moon.

Was it just a dream?
  When we were reaching for a star
    To find our way
      Those happy hours we shared
        Seem oh so far away
          And now our days
            Seem lonelier by far.

All too soon it ends, and we are standing here
  Not knowing what to do
    And nothing left to say
      Oh wasted years.

Time goes on and on
　And we are left
　　With only broken memories.
　　　Why doesn't love remain
　　　　The same always?
　　　　　Why should we have to lose the ecstasies
　　　　　Of Summer Love.

Passing Years

Another year gone by and feeling older
The love I felt for you growing colder by the hour
Each day bringing new emptiness
Trying to reach out to you, but touching
Only a vast nothingness.

You've gone into a world that's all your own
Hardly speaking ... never showing little intimacies
Or secret glances, no special warmth
From fingers touching secretly
But maybe knowing ... love will soon be gone.

Is it possible to change so much
Through passing years and time

I can't remember when your eyes
Last looked in mine
And I could tell by looking
That you loved me.

Love's End

Take me in your arms, and love me one more time,
Press your lips to mine, and say you care
Just for old time's sake, we'll love the night away,
I have so much love for you to share.

Not so long ago, I meant the world to you,
As we planned our lives and future years,
Now your plans have changed, you found somebody new,
Please don't leave me now, with only tears.

Memories and dreams are all you're leaving me,
How can I go on without you dear?
Don't leave me alone to face the lonely night.
Please don't walk away, I need you here.

So kiss me once again, and darling. Let's pretend
Love has just begun ... Please won't you stay.
Hold me in your arms, before the curtain falls,
And when daylight comes, we'll end the Play.

Open The Door

We hear a knock upon the door
    But, heedless, turn away,
        We hear a voice, but hearken not
            And no attention pay.

Just pause a while before you take
    Your path of Wayward Sin,
        We knock again, so open up
            The door, and let him in.

I Need Your Love

I need your love to help me through the night,
Your arms around me until the morning light,
So please come back, you know where you belong,
I need your everlasting love to make me strong.

You found someone new, and left a love that's true,
How can I carry on, to face the lonely dawn,
So darling, please bring back your love to me.
I can't go on this way, my heart will not be free.

So, take my heart, it's no more good to me,

It's broken now, my darling can't you see,

What good is life if dreams will not come true,

Why won't you share my everlasting love for you?

So Much To Offer

"And how are you today?" I asked

Of one who looked so well,

And looking at me, said,

"My life's just Hell.

I've got the flu, and I feel so bad,

There's not a sickness I ain't had,

I'm just not well."

Her friend then said, "Life's such a bore,

There's nothing left for me no more,

Joe's got no job,

We can't survive,

What sense is there to be alive?"

I said Goodbye and went my way

And thought, "It's such a gloomy day,"

And then I met her coming near,

Her coat all shabby, shoes threadbare,

But smiling such a happy smile
Her radiance could span a mile.

"I just got word about my Jim,
The doctor had poor hopes of him,
A week ago he nearly died,"
And while she spoke she almost cried,
"I couldn't bear it all alone,
But now I know he's coming home."

I thought about the other two
Who had so much, but never knew
Just how to live,
Complaints were all they had to give,
She said Goodbye and went her way,
    Her Happiness had made my day.

Father Time

Old Father Time
   I'm begging you
Turn back the clock
      A year or two

That I may see her once again,
Her lovely face unmarked by pain
And say the words I left unsaid
To take her in my arms instead
Of finding fault so many ways.
Just to speak one word of praise
For all she did,
   But I just hid
         My feelings that I had,
      While she was glad
   When I came home. Each day
She went upon her happy way
Doing so much for me
And now I see
      Her everywhere, in every room.

I know she's gone forever
   Leaving me this empty home
      All alone, and knowing
         I can never
            Say, "I Love You,."

Endless Night

The morning dawns, not a moment too soon
The sun breaks through, turning that old moon
Away, and all the doubts and fears
That night time brings.

The daylight hours are not long enough
To keep the shadows, and the rough
Edge of night away.
Too soon the sun will disappear
   And memories take over
      While I just lie awake, and pray.

The Phone Call

I took a chance
    And called you up today
But when I heard your voice
    I couldn't say
A word ... just stood transfixed
    The phone still in my hand
Praying you would not go away.

Your sweet voice said Hello,
    Just as you did before
    I left you all alone
I didn't know how much you cared
And now I stand, without a word
As you hang up the phone.

There Was A Time

There was a time
  When we could say "I love you"
    Never feeling shy or foolish
      Because we said the words
        In front of all to hear
          But now they're seldom said if ever.

And loving words like, "Darling; dear,"
  Are just forgotten
    And we never say them now.
      Can it be that love has gone
        Or is it so long since we've shown
          Our love
That now when we should be together
We've forgotten how to love.

Surprised

You wished me "Happy Birthday"
                    This morning
Even before I was scarcely awake
You looked at me and kissed me,
And I almost cried, nearly died
Because surprises are so very few
At my age.

Time Wars

Time like a never ending stream
Keeps running by
And with each passing year
Brings Happy Memories
Inter-mingled with the sad.
But never anything to spoil
The happiness we had
And shared together.

I would have given anything
To hear you say you love me...
One more time
Just like so long ago
When we were very young
But now I'm
Left with only memories.

Moonlight shining- sending light
To brighten up the corner of the room
Reaching out and touching you
Beside me, knowing soon

You will be gone.
Remembering all the happy times we've had
Those early love-filled years
Just being together with memories
Bringing unshed tears.

Time like a never-ending stream
Keeps running by
And, with each passing year
Brings happy Memories
Intermingled with the sad
But not enough to spoil
The happiness we've had
Each year a souvenir of wealth
That money cannot buy,
And so much love we shared
Just you and I.

Winter

In Winter ... With Fun ... To Jim

In winter I put on my sox
And wear them into bed,
A flannel jacket then I don
To keep me warm instead
Of turning up the heat,
So many bills to meet.

"I'm finished getting ready dear"
In answer to his shout,
"What's keeping you? It's twelve o'clock"
I hear him holler out.

And when he sees me, then he says
"What's that, your Sunday best?
Instead of taking off your clothes
You're in bed fully dressed!:

Sunless

We sat together in the sunless room

Although the sun still shone

But we were so bereft

That even in the warmth, felt cold

Because the one we loved so much

Had gone, and left us feeling so alone.

To Madge

We've been good friends for many years
The two of us together
Sharing laughter, sometimes tears
Through fine and stormy weather.

I don't know where the years have gone
Since first we met and found
That we had much in common
As we walked our "Common Ground."

I always knew if you felt 'blue.'
With something on your mind
And sometimes you reached out to me
When I needed someone kind.

We soon will go our separate ways
As we live our lives apart
Knowing there will be a change
As we give 'life' a new start.

What can I say to you today
We both are wondering why
Our lives must change, as we say farewell
But will never say "Good Bye."

Winter

Winter snow, falling oh so white
 And clean upon the earth below,
  Covering the trees with downy blankets
  Making everything a wondrous show
    Of Winter Magic.

Children running with their sleighs
 Cheeks all rosy, laughing all the way
  Up the hill.
   And at the top, stand still
    Breathless, before they climb aboard
    Merrily starting on their way.

     Happy little faces, glowing cheeks, runny noses
      Eyes shining with excitement
       Over the new sleigh from Santa Claus
       And so they keep sliding
        Playing in the snow, because
          They never dream of "Somewhere else to go."

Winter Moonlight

A night too beautiful for words
  Full moon shining on the slightly drifting snow,
    And myriads of stars, sparkling along the Milky Way
      Leaving a breath taking silence on the earth below.

This beauty should go on
  And last forever; but too soon
    The morning dawns, and darkness disappears
      Taking all the sparkling jewels
        And hiding them inside the waning moon.

Twilight Years

Suddenly it dawns
  The morning we have tried
    Successfully for years
      To put aside.

Not wanting life
  To pass us by
    We lived each day
      And tried to hide

The fears we felt
  At growing old
    And love grown cold
      What foolish pride

Kept us from seeing
  There's much more
    To Life, than
      Always keeping score

The quiet years
  Are here at last
    The busy ones
      Forever past

We have to try
  And maybe could
    Enjoy our lives
      The way we should.

Being Alive

What a glorious day
    To be alive you say
But then any day is good to be alive
    To watch the morning sun
Arise with all its splendor
    Starting a new and wonderful day.

Even the rain
    Against the window pane
Playing its happy song, if you only listen
    Just long enough to hear its melody
Beating life's rhythm
    For you and me.

Glorious summer fun

 And lots of playful sun

For everyone to share

 And little children everywhere

Are tanned with happy faces

 Laughing eyes, so much

Wealth to share.

Autumn skies and breezes

 Even sneezes from the flowers

Gone to seed

 And blowing pollen all around

Everything we need, watching

 Clouds drift for hours.

Then comes the snow

 And all we know

Are noises of ski-doos; snowshoes, skis

 Ice skating, Christmas, Santa Claus, all these

Mingled with love,

 What joy to share.

All sent from One above.

Sleep

The hours of darkness seem to never end
Stretching out in lonely solitude to cover me
Bringing little doubts and fears
That seem so mountainous, though only small
If only sleep would come
And end them all.

Not In Vain

Everywhere so dark and dismal
I reach out and find abysmal
Loneliness. No where to turn
No love to lean on, or give
Me strength to carry on.
I yearn
For love, to help me live.

Not much to ask for in this life
This world so empty, torn with strife
Just hold my hand once more
And look into my eyes again
The way you did those days before
And say, our love was not in vain.

Resolutions

Another year gone by
      Replaced by the New
            And Resolutions, that before the year is through
                  Will fall along the Wayside
                        Forgotten like the year before
                              And no one will ask "Why."

Ode To Me

Can that be me? I ask
      Who once was young and full of life
            Not caring what tomorrow held in store
                  Just asking to be a little older
                        And eager to enjoy so much more.

Everything was Oh so wonderful
      Awakening each new dawn with so much zest
            Happy to be alive ... no worry
                  Only seeing in life and everyone
                        The very best.

But, Oh! The years have gone
    Not even knowing how, or caring,
        Raising children, and not having time
      For nonsense, only sharing
        Everything with them.

Bringing them up the way we should
    Praying they will mold good
      And useful lives, and then
        They grew up all too fast and when

I had more time at last
    To be myself again
      They all had gone and I was left alone
      And lonely,

Wondering if my life had been in vain.

Rememb'ring

I keep remembering all the things
    You said my dear
      When I was near you,
        The way your lips curved into
      That handsome smile
        I love so well.

Even the little laugh wrinkles
     Around your eyes
          That seemed to tell
               You smiled a lot
                    And lips that formed the words
                         I Love You.

The color of your hair, your eyes
     The way you walk,
          And when you leave
               The way I miss you
                    Everything about you
                         Makes me crave to
                              Kiss you.

Home Again

I hear the whistle of the wind
Rustling through the leaves,
And wonder where you are tonight
Or if your poor heart grieves.

As mine does, now that you are gone
To satisfy your mind
With travel, as you go your way
Leaving my heart behind.

You left without a last farewell
A kiss, or fond embrace
You never even saw the teardrops
Shining on my face.

You traveled on, but finding not
The Quest you ventured for,
Returned back home, and here at last
Found true love at your door.

Hopeful

I'd like to hear your voice once more
    And see you
        As you looked before
            You Left

My Love for you
    I'd not reveal
        You didn't realize

I could feel

Bereft

I still remember

How you'd smile

And I would linger

All the while

With you

You then made mention

We must part

You never knew

You left my heart

So blue

I tried to win you

Back again

You didn't know

My heart remained

So True

You then came back

I had to cry

For joy, you found

At last that I

Loved you.

Turmoil

The world is in turmoil today
And many mothers kneel and pray,
For sons, who, in this war-torn strife
Now seek to take each comrade's life,
Chaotic ... What will be its fate
This world of envy ... cruel hate.

The sword to us was thrown, that we
Might hold it high, and ever be
Loyal, faithful, and always shield
The rights of those who ever sleep
   In Flanders Field.

The Stars

The stars in the heaven
   Look down from above,
The moon sends its gleam on the
   Glittering snow
And young people hand in hand
   So much in love
Whisper sweet nothings
   In voices soft and low.

Old Friends

I see the old school on the hill
So many years ago; but still
I can remember every face
As we were then, so young
     and not a trace
of worry , only happiness , and fun.
So many friends,
     I wonder where they've gone.

Solitaire

The lonely hours have come again
    There's darkness everywhere.
Wind howling, and the falling rain
    Making hollow music
While I'm playing Solitaire.

Sleep just won't come, and fill my head
    With happy dreams, and so
I stay awake instead,
    And think, if only
Loneliness would go.

Loneliness

What is this feeling?

    So Bereft,

So lonely ... even in a crowd

    A suffocating feeling ... gasping

Reaching out to touch someone

    But finding only Abysmal emptiness.

Love

Love is shown

    So many ways

        Never alone

            Just spending days

                Together.

Counting the hours

    When I'm away

        Sending flowers

        Just to say

            "I Love You."

My Treasures

A Bible filled with memories
Of all your growing years
Treasures neatly folded
So many souvenirs

Of happy days when you were young
And starting on your own
To go to school, your first reports,
My ,how the Years have flown

I've kept so many little things
You did for me each year
Your cards for Mother's days gone by
To me they are so dear.

Each Christmas card is put away
And Anniversaries too.
Easter cards, and Valentines
Each one a part of you.

And so I'll keep my souvenirs
From each of you a part
Too precious to be thrown away
And so dear to my heart.

The Worrier

You worry over little things
You tell me every day
Bad weather makes you feel so sad
Nothing ever makes you glad.
You're in an awful way.

It's pills for this
And pills for that
Afraid to eat, you may get fat.
Arthritis pain keeps you awake
Another pill you have to take.

Sunshine isn't good for you
And so you stay inside
Your room all summer, listening to
The dreary news or watching soaps,
Or reading the TV Guide.

Today, it's something else that's wrong
A cough, a cold, a sneezing bout.
Everyday, the same old song
Enough to wear a body out.

Mixing up another brew
For your constipation
The bathroom is so busy
It's like Grand Central Station.

The dark clouds hover over you
Hiding all your Wealth
You always see the Gloomy View
While enjoying your "Poor Health."

Success

The road may be wrong
As you travel along
And your burdens too heavy to bear.
The top of the mountain
Looks so far away
And you wonder if any one cares.

Hold on to your dreams
Don't hide them away
Keep climbing, look forward, don't stop

Today, or tomorrow, who knows,
One more step
Will bring you, at last,
To the top.

Dusk

Mother's day

Another Mother's Day gone by.
Why couldn't you have wished me love,
Or kissed my cheek, I waited 'till
The day had gone, and still
Not one endearing word of love.

No roses, no bouquet of any flowers
Were in an array, no little card
Remembering all the hours
I shared with you in all those years
So many times you've left so much unsaid
Which I keep silent with my tears unsaid.

Life is filled with Happy Memories
Of days we share
With those we love.

The days are flying by
And I can't tell sometimes
What day it is, or if there's something special
I forgot to do.
They say we're in our twilight years
And I know why
We're in a Twilight zone – we two.

Birthday

You could have spoken
  But you left the words unsaid.
    Missing your chance so many times.
      Too proud – Too obstinate – Too much a man?
        Forgetting to be a father to that grown-up
          "Little girl at heart"
            WAITING – to hear
              You say before the day is over,
                "Happy Birthday Dear"

Uptight

Why so many different moods?
  Sometimes so happy, then so
    Uptight, in just a minute.
      You change your ways, your eyes
        Betray your feelings
          This hatred I see,
            Is it at the world around you,
              Or just me?

The days are slipping by so quickly,
Days that should be filled with love
And laughter, and joy we should be sharing
But you go on your way never caring
How your attitude affects those who
Love and care.

If you could for just a minute
Find the time to search in your heart
To see what's in it ... What lies ahead
For you and me ... What unfilled dreams
Unspoken words of love, if only said
Before we leave for the UNKNOWN
And all is Dead.

My Love

Oh, I'd love to see him more
Than I ever have before,
For I never do get tired when he's near
He just drives away my cares,
When I'm sad, my heart he cheers
And when I say "I love Him".
I'm sincere.

Wistful

I'd like to hold your hand again
And walk along the moon filled path,
The snow clad hill
To feel your warmth, your love that covered me
And made my heart stand still.

It was so very long ago,
But really just a dream
That old ski trail we walked along,
The trees all filled with snow
That fell so softly all around,
And filled my heart with song.

Yesterday and Tomorrow

'I'd trade all of my tomorrows'
For just one yesterday
Just to have you here beside me
And you'd never go away
All the lonely hours of waiting
Arid the sleepless nights I've known
I'm so tired of being left here
On my own

All the years we were together

Never dreaming they would end

That same day you'd leave, without 'goodbye'

Or having time to mend

The many bridges that were broken

And the promises we made

Or the unkind words that

Sometimes made me cry.

That tomorrows don't mean anything

Compared to yesterday

I just sit here in the evening

When the shadows come to stay

All night long I keep remembering

Memories never go away

And tomorrow will be lost

In yesterday.

To My Children

(All Five of You)

I keep a special place within my heart

For every one of you.

Although at times, you seem so far apart,

Each little space, keeps you together No harsh or unkind words

are ever said

And even though you do not spend

Unspoken words are kinder,

And whenever I feel

The need to reach out to you

     I know that you are near

     Within the words, that confine

     Each one of you, to me, so dear

     And keep you close to me

          Forever.

A Prayer On Being Thankful

Oh Lord, I pray
Help me to face another day,
I know you have so much to do
So many people asking you
To help them in their time of need
And others, who, in selfish greed
keep asking you to send them more,
Without a thought of all the poor
Who need so much; but only ask
For just enough to face the task
Of barely living every day,
Needing you to show the way,
That they may face another dawn,
Not knowing how to carry on.
Barely enough to keep alive
Or help their little ones survive.
We have so much; but have we tried
To let you know we're satisfied?
We never make their burdens light
Don't even match the "Widow's mite."

Whatever will become of us?

Who knowingly make so much fuss

About the little things gone wrong

When we should raise each voice in song

To thank you for our happy days

And lift our hearts in grateful praise

That we are not the World's Oppresses.

We're lucky, Lord, That you have blessed

So many of us, here on Earth.

Be thankful that you gave us birth,

To live each day, the way we should.

 Why not help others to feel good?

 If we would only do our best

Then maybe we would all be blest

And never have to kneel and say

"Help us Lord, to face the day."

Night Nears

&

Parting Scuffs

&

Jigs & Reels

&

Things Political

is also

What I leave behind.

It's the week of Aunt Eileen Powell's 90th birthday.

I asked if there was anything she'd like. Turns out she and Caren & myself all felt there were still a few poems to add. So we're able to give Eileen the gift she wanted – for this edition contains all the poems she wants in her book.

To celebrate this poet's 90th birthday, we issue this edition, with thanks to a glorious Aunt for the greatest gift she could give us – and that's her presence in the world.

We begin with her political verses about various leaders of Newfoundland. Of talk show hosts, and...well, anyone who she felt might be too bigoty – too proud of themselves.

Oh yes, she is not a fan of patriarchal songs...

Answer To Paul Anika

Having your baby,

I'm a woman half dead

 And my eyes are red from crying.

Having your baby, I'm afraid to live

And I'm so afraid of dying.

When you heard the "good news"

You said you were leaving

With the future bleak,

I could hardly speak for grieving,

Little seed inside me,

I can feel it growing

You couldn't care less

When you said that you were going.

Having your baby,

You are long since gone

But I'll carry on, without you

Having your baby.

You were such a heel, I don't give

A damn about you,

I can keep on trying,

Just to go on living

When the baby comes you can bet that you'll be giving

Lots of child support, if I can only catch you,

You are such a cad,

 there is no one else to match you.

Having your baby.

I can keep on trying,

Just to go on living

When the baby comes you can bet that you'll be giving

Lots of child support, if I can only catch you,

You are such a cad,

 there is no one else to match you.

Having your baby.

To Ron Pumphey on Open Line

Speak on, dear Ron. Your voice drones on
Your accent loud and clear
You rant and shout, without a doubt,
At things you loath to hear.

You're sweet as pie, you almost cry
You put on quite a show
For people who look up to you
And bouquets to you throw.

There are a few, quite wise to you
The educated ones
Your reprimands, they just can't stand
And no use for your puns.

You sit and chaff, and gaily laugh
At things these people say.
Both day and night, their sorry plight
Keeps you so blithe and gay.

Put on your show, you and I know
How well you like to scoff,
But when I hear your voice so clear
I turn the button off.

Hallelujah To Our Brian

Hallelujah to our Brian
We'll be living on Orion
Don't be fooled by all they lying
While his truth is marching on.

Hallelujah to The Party

They are the Liberal Party
And they have a special plan
To bring new hope and glory
To the shores of Newfoundland
They're going out from door to door
To gather every vote
For the plans they have in store.

Glory, Glory, lets stay healthy
Life with Brian will be wealthy
No more worries for our Island
Just you wait and see
(How stupid can we be?)

We'll have no health care worries
Unemployment will be gone
They're going to bring our people back
To sing a happy song
He tells us there will be a job
For every living one
His truth is marching on.

Glory to the unemployment
Every dollar will be well spent
To older people comes enjoyment
Their lives will be content.

Our nurses are all overworked
Our health care's gone to pot
But Brian just evades it all
And says look what we've got
Sure, Voiseys Bay and all our deals
Will put an end to that
Just walk right up and vote
Glory, glory for our leader
Never worry about the future
He can solve it all by trying
To sneak out the back door.

We've heard so many promises

How can we keep the score

So come on Mr. Premier

We're waiting here for more.

Where is the money coming from?

It was all gone before

We reached the polling door!

And she is constant, her poems about war remember those who died. Every Remembrance Day she remembers.

Princess Anne arrived from England this year, and shook hands with and met our poet. All who meet her know that Aunt Eileen remembers exactly what most needs to be remembered; how the very people who fought for us, became marginalized as they aged...

England's Call

The twelfth of May, on Mother's day,

A sad day for us all

Our boys went out to fight the foe

And answer Britain's call.

The streets were thronged' there was no song

Of laughter, joy, or mirth

They went in aid of England

The land which gave them birth.

But why should we remain so sad?

Our boys were full of laughter.

They nodded greetings, and called out,

"It's Hitler, Mom, we're after.

We're hoping soon to see you

To your safe return we look.

We trust that God will keep you

Brave lads of Corner Brook.

Tune to Londonderry Air

Oh Danny Boy. The elderly are falling
Beside the way, our hopes and dream laid bare.
We want to see a Bright and Happy "Golden Life"
Good healthy years and tender loving care.

We're looking for a future
That will be "stress free"
With Hope and Joy, for us all to share
And when we reach our Golden, final years of Life
We hope and pray, Oh Danny Boy
For us, you will be there.

□

Elder's College
(Tune of Squid Jigging ground)

We've been together for six days already
My how the time flies when
You're having such fun.
Tween eatin' and learnin'
We're all instant scholars
By the time we get home, bys
We'll weigh half a ton.

Our teachers have patience
And keep our attention
Although now and then Men
Will have a quick nod,
While Ida keeps asking our Richard such questions
That we know by her knowledge
She came from our sod.

With 'hexperts' on music
We've learned about 'Oprey'
And Bach and 'Broke"
With M and M scales
We thank our Wayne Rodgers
Who taught us old codgers
About music notes with their squiggly tails.

New "Hart" was a subject
That caught our attention.
Those pictures were something
To ponder about.
Paul Hudson and teacher
Would have made a fine preacher
If only we could have taught him
How to shout.

Now, Betty from Ontario
Played piano
And Arthur and Jim had some slides
That they showed
Where Lillian, Dorothy, both did the line dance
And Anna Marie sang our Newfoundland Ode.

There were Lottie and Edith and Winifred Fisher
And Harvey and Pat and Elizabeth too.
John, Gina and Nadine and Newfoundland's Edna,
And Clara and Ernest made up half the crew.

We can't forget Thora, and Thelma and Nancy,
Believe it or not, we had two Edwards too.
With Irene and Lillian who was our poet
And wouldn't you know it, there still was a few.

Like Mary Jane Elkins and Jessica Woodcock
A Dorothy, Donald and also a Jim
Gertie and Eileen were from Bay of Islands
Surrounded by water, a good place to swim.

We have special mention for Christine, our Captain,
And Debbie and Maud, Steve and cute Lori too.
We had such a good time, it won't be the last time
That we Elder Hostlers make up the crew!

□ &

I asked if there was any song that she wrote to her own inner music, that would speak to each reader. Some piece of advice...

There was, and we wish to close this birthday add-on to her book, with the clear Alto tone of Eileen Powell as she sings directly to each of us bringing hope-light to a shadowed age & say...never give up; hold fast to what your own life tells you.

Success

The road may be wrong

As you travel along

And your burdens too heavy to bear.

The top of the mountain

Looks so far away

And you wonder if any one cares.

Hold on to your dreams

Don't hide them away

Keep climbing, look forward, don't stop

Today, or tomorrow, who knows,

One more step

Will bring you, at last,

To the top.

The Next Book for "Newfoundland Press" & our 'Lost & Found' series will be:

"Doctor Jim: Life & Death"

We join Dr. Jim Gough as World War Two seemed like it would go on forever, and then hear him as he graduates, & see him decide to return to the place he loved best in the World - his native Newfoundland. Funny, irreverent , and a fierce defender of all patients.

"Doctor Jim: Life & Death" - will be our next release.   His story in his own words.

And there's a Free E- Book at Bookrix :

Gramp's War: Letters From The Front

http://www.bookrix.com/_ebook-william-gough-gramp-039-s-war/

When my Grandfather Gough enlisted to fight and left his home Outport of Elliston, Newfoundland in WW 1, he was a innocent boy. By the end of WW 1 he was a shattered man, who had lost the main illusions of his life. Yet, he managed to write brave letters from the front; letters that reflected his life and times in such a way that I want what he said to be available for free, for us all - so we may all avoid war in all times forever.

www.ingramcontent.com/pod-product-compliance
Lightning Source LLC
Chambersburg PA
CBHW032006040426
42448CB00006B/503